VICTORY Thru SURRENDER

Breaking the Stronghold of Food on your Life....

by

Pauline Porter M.A.

Copyright 2019- Pauline D. Porter M.A.

All rights reserved. This book is protected by the copyright laws of the United States of America. This book may not be copied or reprinted for commercial gain or profit. The use of short quotations or occasional page copying for personal or group study is permitted and encouraged. Permission will be granted upon request.

Unless otherwise identified, Scripture quotations are taken from the Amplified Bible. Copyright 1965 by the Zondervan Publishing. Please note that the name satan and related names are not capitalized. We choose not to acknowledge him, even to the point of violating grammatical rules.

ISBN: 978-0-578-21718-5

VICTORY

Thru

SURRENDER

CONTENTS

Forward

Introduction

Chapter 1: My story at least some of it
Chapter 2: We are in a war
Chapter 3: Vanity really
Chapter 4: Getting honest
Chapter 5: What is a STRONGHOLD
Chapter 6: A reward, I don't think so.
Chapter 7: Childhood
Chapter 8: Focus
Chapter 9: Diet books.........Nooooooooo
Chapter 10: Dying to self
Chapter 11: Take it back!
Chapter 12: Feeling sorry for ourselves
Chapter 13: Overcomers
Chapter 14: Made for more
Chapter 15: Disciplined commitment
Chapter 16: Growing closer to God
Chapter 17: Turn it over
Chapter 18: Where is the trust
Chapter 19: Trust and believe
Chapter 20: Fear

Chapter 21: John 10:10
Chapter 22: How
Chapter 23: Holy Spirit
Chapter 24: Greatest days
Chapter 25: Surrender first step
Chapter 26: Power
Chapter 27: Talk to yourself
Chapter 28: The real battlefield
Chapter 29: I can do this
Chapter 30: Silencing the cries
Chapter 31: Final note

INTRODUCTORY

This is not another diet book. As we know diets don't work. This is a book God helped me write because he does not want us to be bound up by STRONGHOLDS in our life, especially with food.

He said in His Word, he wants us to live an abundant life, and I think that means, no I don't think I know that means he wants us to be free of anything that holds us back from being the best you can be.

The thief comes only to steal and kill and destroy; I came That they may have life, and have it abundantly.
John 10:10

If you believe for some reason God doesn't care about that stronghold food has on you, you are wrong. He wants us to live a life of freedom, not in bondage to food. He wants us to be healthy to be able to serve Him. He wants our focus to be on Him not food. But, for a lot of us food is the center of our life.

Are you ready for the challenge? Or, would you rather just take the easy way out and stay where you are. How's that working for you so far? I believe you are ready since you picked up this book. God is talking to you even now and He will speak to you through this book just as he spoke to me in my heart as I was writing it.

Another new diet will NOT help you take off the weight and to permanently keep off the weight if that is what you want. You must break the STRONGHOLD food has on your life and by doing this, things will finally begin to fall into place in your life. You will find yourself eating more healthy foods and it will be effortless. It is as simple as asking God what he thinks you should eat, after all he is the one who created us so who better to know what is best for us. Then there is the issue of what we need to do to be obedient to what he tells us. This is where the problem comes in.

Sometimes like the man in John 5:5-6, who had suffered for 38 years, we need to ask ourselves as Jesus ask this man, "Do you want to become well?" Are you really in earnest about getting well? If so then let's take this journey together with God, and have VICTORY thru SURRENDER!

GOD BLESS YOU:

P.S. You are going to need a journal as you go through this book so you can WRITE ABOUT IT. You may discover some things about yourself as you do this that you did not even realize.

CHAPTER ONE

My story, at least some of it.

Just like those of you who are now reading this book, I have struggled all my life with my relationship with food. No I'm not just someone writing a book, I know where you are coming from. I know your pain, the feelings of failure. The feeling of never being able to get this emotional eating under control.

I too have been on about every diet out there and I have a shelf full of books telling how and what I need to do to lose weight and keep it off. Each one promising me great results. Each one telling me this is good for me to eat or drink and the next book says don't eat or drink that under any circumstances. No wonder we are all so confused and then finally just throw up our hands and say, I'VE HAD IT!!! I'm eating what I want when I want and that is that! I don't care how much I gain, God loves me whether I'm fat or skinny. Yes he does but he also wants us healthy.

Then there are these so called simple recipes. REALLY! Then they try to sell you on how good they are. Mind you some are. You will see them in an ad tasting the food and just falling all over themselves telling you how good that food is. My guess is that they are eating something that looks like the food in the recipe, but it is made totally different. What they are eating is actually good.

They will also try to tell you how these foods are going to fill you up. Well, they have never met someone who is dealing with the STRONGHOLD of food in their life. What they don't realize is we don't eat for pleasure, we are eating to stuff something down we don't want to deal with and it usually will take a lot of food to do that.

That was me for many years. Using food to stuff down the pain of my childhood. I learned to do this at a very early age. I had a wonderful grandma who could cook and bake anything. Oh my, I can smell her kitchen even now as I write this. She felt somewhat helpless to help me at home, so her solution was to bake and allow me to eat what I wanted, because she saw how much I loved what she would make just for me. It was her way of showering love.

I was lucky to like to spend time out doors with Papa, otherwise if I was like some of the kids I see today inside playing computer games all the time, heaven only knows I could be as big as a house, but I think being active outside helped me.

Then as an adult, I realized I had some issues to deal with. The food could only push the hurt down and fill the hole inside of me for so long. When I finally hit a brick wall with all of this I decided or rather God did, to go into counseling. God had a friend of mine to introduce me to a Christian Counselor and then I began my new journey. It was one of the hardest most painful times in my life, but, it was also one of the best and yes I would do it all over again to get where I am today. My healing did not come over night, and it is still going on, but in a more positive way now.

During this journey, God began to reveal to me that my focus was more on food healing my pain then on Him. He was right of course. I had to learn to trust him, to give my pain and the healing process to him. Again I need to stress this doesn't happen overnight, it has been a process, but one that even today just keeps bringing me closer to Him.

Sometimes God will break a STRONGHOLD that you have, be it food, shopping, drugs, sex, whatever it may be very quickly and there are other times he may not because he wants you to grow stronger and he wants to stretch you to learn something through it all. This seems to be the case for me. Yes, I have changed a great deal, Yes, I still have times of wanting my old comfort foods. I have learned that that's okay too because food no longer has a STRONGHOLD on me God does.

So take the lessons you will learn from this book, spend time with God and begin to focus more on him then your food. Yes, he will help you to do this. Be patient with yourself, take one day at a time. You won't regret it. God has blessed me so much in my journey with him and I know he will do the same for you. He loves you too much to leave you frustrated and believing the lies of satan, and feeling like a failure. He wants you to see and to love yourself the way he does. He also wants you to use this book and His Word (the Bible) as a part of your healing process.

WRITE ABOUT IT……..

After reading this first chapter, write your story in your journal.

Are your feelings similar to the ones I was having?

CHAPTER TWO

We are in a war.

We are engaged in a war for our health, and the enemy is none other than satan. The mind is where the battlefield happens to be because that is the only place satan can try to get to us. He finds our weakest link and believe me he knows all of them, and then him and his friends go to work on us. Our mind is where he begins to set up our STRONGHOLDS. The devil is smart, he works hard to know all you are vulnerable to, and then he will make his well laid plans to try to bring us down.

We have STRONGHOLDS in our mind that satan set up at a very early age. Things in childhood that we liked, like grandmas baking started to stick with me even as a kid. It was comfort to me.

We can win the victory over satan in our lives by quoting scripture and keeping it in our hearts to call up when an attack of satan comes. For example: here is one of those scriptures:

> *If you abide in My Word (hold fast to my teachings and live in accordance with them), you are truly my my disciples. And you will know the Truth, and the Truth will set you free.*
> *John 8:31-32*

It is very important to renew our minds on a daily basis with God's Word. This is not a onetime thing, because satan is always trying to take us down by using and working on our weakest link, FOOD! Also read and study on II Corinthians 10:4-5. The weapon of God's Word is the only thing that can and will defeat satan and the STRONGHOLD of food in your life or any other STRONGHOLD you may have. You will need to refocus your mind from food to Jesus and His food for you. Refocusing your mind is one of the **keys to having VICTORY over your food STRONGHOLD.** As we begin to release ourselves, in other words get ourselves out of God's way and start trusting Him, we will gain the confidence to do what needs to be done to be successful.

Jesus is always ready to fulfil His promises to us. He wants us to have victory in all areas of our life, but we must be willing to walk the whole way with Him. And this is the way:

> *For no temptation (no trial regarded as enticing to sin, has overtaken you and laid hold on you that is not common to man that is, not adjusted and adopted and belonging to human experience, and such as man can bear) but God is faithful (to His Word and to His compassionate nature), and He (can be trusted) not to let you be tempted and tried and assayed beyond your ability and strength of resistance and power to endure, but with the temptation He will (always) also provide the way out (the means of escape to a landing place) that you may be capable and strong and powerful to bear up under it patiently.*
> *I Corinthians 10:13*

Our outside behavior is only because of what is going on inside of us. The attitudes and thoughts about ourselves that we have grown up with. Satan knows these thoughts and uses them against us. So we need to find the negative root and destroy it with God's Word. Satan wants to be able to control what we think about, that is how he can then control our actions. But God! He is on our side fighting for us. Keep your eyes on Him and Your heart and mind filled with His Word and satan will be defeated!

When we sin by overeating does that mean we are expressing our preference for something other than God? YES! We most certainly are saying that God and his way are less satisfying than the way of sin. What we are doing is exchanging God's glory for another glory. Which is far from being satisfying.

Nothing will be different until you think differently. You need a desire to change your thoughts then you need to take action to get to the place where you can think God's thoughts..

Do you want to think differently? Do you want to do things in a different healthy way to improve your life and health?

When you get set free you will need someone to help you walk in that freedom or you can fall back into the familiar of the past. It is always a good idea to have someone be it a Christian Counselor, family member or friend to keep you accountable.

WRITE ABOUT IT

What are some of the things you ran to for comfort as a child? (like my grandmas baking).

Do you still go to whatever it is for comfort?

What were some of your thoughts about yourself as a child.

CHAPTER THREE

Vanity really

It is not all about vanity. Sure we want to look good and feel good in our clothes, but more importantly we need to take care of the body God has given us. After all it is His home. I think sometimes we forget or prefer to ignore that fact. Especially when all we want to do is satisfy our flesh.

How many of you can say, my plan is not working. If you are reading this today, then God is moving in this area of your life. He is telling you it is time for a lifestyle change. God wants and needs you to be healthy, why well, #1. Because he loves you and #2. To be able to do the work he has called you to do. Is the Lord putting His finger on any area of your life, if so you need to respond to him now.

Satan is smart, he knows our weaknesses and he will use them to set up strongholds in our lives. He knows we will desire what we focus on, so instead of focusing on food you need to focus more on God to feed you. Because, the more truth we have in our hearts the more able we will be to break those STRONGHOLDS of food!

If you are still struggling with temptation maybe you need to ask this question of yourself: Is it possible that I love and rely on food to comfort me more than God? Hummmmm food for thought (no pun intended).

The answer to that question can be a rude awakening. But it is time to be honest with yourself and probably with God. Yes, we hate admitting this, but it is necessary to be able to be set free. For too long we have avoided or lived in denial.

Psalm 78:18 says, and they tempted God in their hearts by asking for food according to their (selfish) desire and appetite. God never intended for us to want things like food more than Him.

As we keep running to food, it becomes our so called place of safety. Then satan takes control and begins to make this a STRONGHOLD in our lives. He will tell us lies like; You will feel so much better by eating this. Or I should be able to eat whatever I want to help me feel better.

The Bible tells us in Romans 12:2, that we are transformed by the renewing of our minds. This is true of anything in our lives we want to change. I know this sounds simple, but it is not. It takes a lot of work to rid our minds of the lies satan has placed there over the years, but we know that nothing is impossible with God. God wants us to run to Him for help. He knows and understands we cannot break these STRONGHOLDS in our lives on our own. We need to lean on and TRUST Him. God wants to be our STRONGHOLD of PROTECTION. As we study, meditate, and just stay in His Word, His Word will slowly but powerfully begin to change you. We cannot just visit the Word occasionally and think we can change. No, it takes time and study in the Word. We need to live in the Word, and allow God to work in a very powerful way in our lives, as only he can do.

If we are obedient and taking this time with God, it can change not only our thinking, but our whole life. It will even change the way we think about ourselves. We will begin to see ourselves as God sees us, not the critical way we look at ourselves.

WRITE ABOUT IT

If you are a born again Christian, how do you feel about your body being the home of God?

Does it make you think more about what you put in your body?

CHAPTER FOUR

Getting honest

One of the things we need to do is to get honest with ourselves. So often we just gloss over the reality that is staring us right in the face. It is so easy to convince ourselves that I deserve that treat of candy, cake or whatever you are craving because you have had a tough day. Wonder what would happen if you started craving God more than that food for comfort. How would your Spirit feel? How do you feel after you have indulged in your comfort food? Maybe good for a bit tell the guilt sets in and you then want more to get rid of that feeling and on and on. How do you think you would feel if you went to God's Word for comfort instead??? Maybe it is time to try it!

Read and study the story of the rich man (Mark 10: 17-31). He was unable to give up riches, (his comforts) to follow Jesus. Some of us have been the same way with our overeating. Do you think you can give up your riches in food and follow Jesus and look to Him for comfort instead?

This battle is in 3 areas of our lives: Spiritual, physical, and mental.

We need to seek God to empower us to have a spiritual want to, to break our STRONGHOLDS. As for physically, we need to realize that what we put in our bodies does matter to God, and our health.

We were created to desire God not food, but satan wants to replace our desire for God with food. Satan tries hard to lure us away from loving God and listening to Him

PRAYER
"Father, I recognize that I'm fearfully and wonderfully made and you have made me a steward over my health and my body. I lay this body on the altar of faith. With your help and strength, this STRONGHOLD of food is broken off of me. God, I receive it. I am well and healthy and strong. "I am not hungry". I tell my body when to be hungry and when to eat. In you I am an OVERCOMER! Thank you Father. In Jesus Name. Amen

We need to remember that overeating is sin. Read and study these verses:

I Corinthians 6:12
I Corinthians 10:7
Philippians 3:19-20
Proverbs 23:1-3
Proverbs 23:19-21
Romans 14:13-17

We also need to remember the following:
1. My worth is not determined by what a
   a scales says.

2. Who I am on the inside is much more
   Important than who I am on the outside.

3. I don't need to live up to what others think,
   I only need to believe God's truth about me.

We need to be honest with ourselves about how we feel when people judge us. We need to learn to not let others bother us. Instead, release them and pray for them. We need to learn to see ourselves through our Heavenly Fathers eyes only. This is the honest view of who we are. God wants us to see ourselves through His eyes and He cares a lot more about our character than our appearance.

Satan wants to destroy us and he will use whatever means he can to do this. He does his best to get our eyes off of Jesus and our thoughts too. But just remember He that is in me is stronger than he that is in the world. Stop judging yourself as well, learn to love yourself as our wonderful Jesus does. No power other than the power of Jesus can overcome you.

WRITE ABOUT IT

After a tough day and say you have given into temptation for your favorite comfort food how do you feel after awhile?

Good or Guilty and why?

CHAPTER FIVE

What is a STRONGHOLD

Strongholds are fortified patterns of thinking that are stubbornly resistant to God's Word and will for us.

Dr. Charles Stanley shows how strongholds develop. They begin with a thought. One thought becomes a consideration, a consideration develops into an attitude, which leads then to action. Action repeated becomes a habit, and a habit establishes a "power base for the enemy," that is a STRONGHOLD.

We need to memorize God's Word and allow it to drop into our hearts to fight the temptation of the devil. Jesus was ready when the devil came to tempt Him. When satan would make an enticing proposal, Jesus said, "It is written," and then He went on the offensive with particular Scripture passages. Satan had no choice but to flee.

We must be ready to do the same thing when satan comes after our thoughts. The only way to do that is to study, study, study God's Word!

Withdrawal from foods we are addicted to can be as tough or tougher than withdrawal from drugs. You don't need drugs on a daily basis but you do need food to live.

Is there a certain food you don't think you can live without? There are foods I cannot keep in the house. If I want those I go get enough just to satisfy me.

Try and go at least a week without your favorite comfort food and see how you feel.

Then there is the problem as you sit down to relax in the evening with TV and family. All those food commercials. When you are trying to break your STRONGHOLD on food these are difficult to keep watching because satan will use it to temp you. You may need to switch the channel tell they pass or leave the room. Seeing these images can begin to penetrate your mind and wear down your resolve. This can happen so quickly. It is very necessary to protect ourselves from these kind of temptations as well. Put on God's armor and keep your eyes on Him not the food. Our thoughts influence our behavior and our emotions and this can all influence our health as well. Your emotions are strongly influenced by your thoughts. As you strive to learn how to break the STRONGHOLD food has on you, you will need to think seriously about how your thoughts and emotions affect your eating.

You will also need to take your thoughts captive (see 2Cor.10:5). Whenever you notice your mind drifting and thinking about your comfort foods, take that thought captive right away. You have control over where you let your mind drift too, so do not let it wonder just anywhere it wants to go. Satan loves it when your mind begins wondering since that happens to be his playground where he sits up those STRONGHOLDS. Show him whose boss and boot him out of your mind with God's Word and promises for you. Do whatever it takes with the wisdom God has given to you for you to have VICTORY over your STRONGHOLD.

Steep your mind in the Word of God, just like Job. Job recognized how important it was to meditate on God's Word that is what sustained him. Job said, "I have not departed from the command of His lips; I have treasured the Words of His mouth more than my necessary food" (Job 23:12). We all need to be more like Job and esteem God's Word as much more important than our food.

Our love for God's Word can help us to make choices that enable us to live righteously.

One of the best lessons you can learn to break that STRONGHOLD of food is to stop feeding your desires with food and instead begin to feed your hunger with the Word of God.

When satan tried to tempt Jesus he answered satan in this way: "Man shall not live on bread alone, but on every word that proceeds out of the mouth of God" (Matthew 4:4).

Jeremiah said "Your words were found and I ate them, and your words became a joy to me and the delight of my heart; for I have been called by Your name, O Lord God of hosts. (Jeremiah 15:16). You too can make this statement all you need to do is study and meditate on the best food of all, God's Word.

WRITE ABOUT IT

Do you have a favorite verse to help you in times of temptation? What is it and why or how did this verse catch your heart?

CHAPTER SIX

A reward I don't think so.

We also have mental strongholds we need to break. We need to renew our minds and change the way we think about food. For some of us food is what we run to for comfort rather than God. This needs to change. Our biggest battles are in our minds. That is satans playground.

Sometimes food is or can become our reward. After a tough day you can convince yourself that you deserve that chocolate sunday or candy or whatever you may be craving, but do you deserve the guilt you will feel after eating the food you chose?

There are times when we will use food to stuff the pain from the past down that we have not dealt with. How many of you like myself could set down and polish off a bag of cookies or chips when some of those bad memories start to surface. The bad news is there comes a time when one bag is not enough, you need more, just like what happens with drugs. But because we are Christians we have a tendency to not look at overeating as a sin, but God says it is read the following passages:

> Proverbs 23:20-21
> Proverbs 28:7

Eating more than we need is being a glutton. We seem to want to pass over that term in the Bible. But being a glutton is a sin and not many churches seem to want to teach this. Many of you say well, I have to eat, yes you do but not OVEREAT!

Let's talk a little bit more about guilt feelings. We tend to think of guilt as a negative and something to avoid, but what if we looked at it as a gift from God to bring us to repentance. We need to get a clear picture of God's holiness and His hatred of sin. The STRONGHOLD food has on our lives is a sin because we are eating more than necessary to be and stay healthy and we are not listening to God when he says STOP eating. We get into disobedience then too.

Progress toward change and breaking the STRONGHOLD of food requires us to see our overeating as sin. God poured out His wrath on the Israelites because of their gluttony. Gluttony is a sin just like drunkenness or spending more than you can afford, I'm sure you can think of more sins to place here. We need to realize this or we will not be able to break that STRONGHOLD food has on us.

I don't know about you, but I'm ready to confront the truth and then feel the freedom that, God purchased for you and me!

So when that STRONGHOLD of food comes to visit, you plead with the Holy Spirit to convict you of your gluttonous eating habits. It might be hard at first, because it is hard to admit we are gluttons, but cry out to God to give you the desire to hate this STRONGHOLD food has had on you for so long.

God has the power to give you what you need to break this sinful lifestyle forever. He sees your heart and knows you want to please Him. You need to learn to hate any options that let you try to satisfy your desire outside of God's love. His love is the only thing that will fill the hole within you that you are using food to fill.

I desire to know what God thinks of my eating habits as well as how He tells me to change. I want so much to please him for all he has done for me that I know I don't deserve, but he loves me that much. Sometimes we just need to stop and think about that for awhile. No one cares as much about every part of our lives except God who gave His only Son for us to be free! That also means to be free of our STRONGHOLDS of food. Pause awhile and just let that soak deep into your heart.

WRITE ABOUT IT

Are there any issues from your past that you feel are too painful to deal with? Write about it. Releasing it to God can set you free from the past.

CHAPTER SEVEN

Childhood

Food as a child was given as a reward or sometimes like in my case to keep my mouth shut about something my mother didn't want dad or anyone else to know about. This is how some food addictions start. You will begin to relate the food to how it made you feel good in a bad situation. Unless you confront this, your mind will begin to accept this as normal in your adult life.

When we are tempted PRAY. We need to talk to God especially in those times of temptation. Sometimes all we can do is call out the name of Jesus and that's okay too. He already knows and understands what we are going through but he wants us to fess up to him. If you are really craving one of your favorite foods, PRAY, or yell JESUS. Tell him how you feel at that time and ask him to give you the strength to eat a healthy snack or just drink some water and let His Word be your food. Through prayer, you can lay a path for VICTORY in your life. Prayer can break that STRONGHOLD of food. One day of victory can taste better than any food you crave.

One of the ways we need to change our mindset is to look at this journey as embracing healthy choices, choices we know God would want us to make, and stop thinking we are denying ourselves. We also need to learn mental and spiritual lessons that will equip us on this new journey and equip us for a lifetime of success.

As we begin to change our bad habits and start to give up those unhealthy comfort foods, we can suddenly feel anxious. Believe me satan will come along and test us. He does not want us to be free. This is where a good support group can come in or a friend to help remind us why we are doing this journey. In other words, we need others to help keep us accountable.

Satan does not want you to be successful in this journey, and he will devise schemes to keep you in the pattern of overeating. This is one good reason you need a group or a good Christian friend who will be there when you call and say HELP! Someone who will speak the truth in love and pray for you. It could also be a family member just someone you know you can trust who will not invite you to go get ice cream to make you feel better.

For a lot of us what we think today reflects what our family focused on. For a lot of people food is a reward, but it also can be a comfort.

As you are reading this book, you are in the process of being changed. "Be transformed by the renewing of your mind!" (Romans 12:2). We need to grow up in our knowledge of God and walk with Him in all areas of our life. God has begun a new work in each one of us, and He is faithful to complete the work until He returns. If we are willing to let God break that STRONGHOLD of food in our lives, this means we are daily being transformed into the image of Christ. We need to read His Word on a daily basis so our minds can be renewed and we decide "That's the truth, and anything less than that is not!" It is a choice that we must make.

So much of who we are is determined by what our minds are focused on. There is a constant battle in our minds between walking in the Spirit and walking in the flesh. Which are you going to choose?

I choose to focus on God and let him help me to make the right choices in life to keep me healthy. The choice begins and ends with following God's battle plan for us.

Read and study Romans 8:7-11. This shows you how important it is to be led by the Holy Spirit. Ask God to deliver you from you food problem.

WRITE ABOUT IT

Make a list of friends and or family who you believe will help support you in this new journey.

CHAPTER EIGHT

Focus

Focus on eating healthy not on losing weight. As you do this you will begin to also lose the weight. The problem with most diet books is they are not getting to the core or root of the problem. Your STRONGHOLD. All they do is tell you about the food that they think is good for you or not good for you to be able to lose weight. They focus so much on food, that you can hardly wait to get something to eat! That defeats the purpose of what you are trying to accomplish. They have been focusing on the wrong thing for years. God knows what you are to eat and how much. So ask him, it is that simple. We are the ones who make it so hard, jumping from one new diet to the next rather than allowing God to help us get to the root of why food has become such a STRONGHOLD in our life. When we are jumping from one new diet to the next, it only keeps us focused on food, and satan just loves that.

We need to learn to focus on the good things. Focus on the positive things you have done. Celebrate one day at a time, when you have spent time with God and been obedient to him. Yes, satan will come in and try to disrupt that time, but don't let him. You can do this, and the blessings that will come from spending time with God and being obedient to him is beyond words.

Stop focusing on the past and past mistakes you have made in this area of your life. Don't think about oh this is going to be hard, not if you listen and follow Jesus. Focus on your progress no matter how small it may be and the blessings that are yet to come for your obedience to God. You have the power through Jesus to defeat the devil and rid yourself of this STRONGHOLD once and for all.

Celebrate your progress. No matter how small it may be it is still PROGRESS. One of the main things we need to celebrate is ourselves. Look how God created you. Celebrate the life God has given you. There is only one like you and God loves you so much.

God wants us to celebrate our victories even if we think they are small. This will make the devil angry and I don't know about you, but I love making him upset..and celebrating will also help you break those STRONGHOLDS of food.

Satan will most certainly come against us hard to try and distort our image of about who we are in Christ. He is so afraid we will get a hold of the truth and then our STRONGHOLD will be broken.

The enemy is so fearful of people who know who they are in Christ. Those who are keeping their focus on the Lord and maturing in their spiritual lives. These are the people who will be able to help others break their STRONGHOLDS in life. Because of this satan wars against us. He wants to destroy us before we can destroy his evil works, as long as we keep our focus on God, he promises He "will never leave us nor forsake us" (Heb. 13:5). We can come through every test and trial, and each of the challenges of life VICTORIOUS! Colossians 1:27 says "Christ in you, the hope of glory." As we put our focus on God and spend time in His presence, we will be transformed and yes we will also have VICTORY thru SURRENDER.

WRITE ABOUT IT

List the diets you have been on. Did any of these focus on God and His Word?

CHAPTER NINE

Diet books------NOOOOOOOO

Most diet books don't get to the ROOT of the problem. This is why so many people will go on a program and lose weight only after a time they begin to gain it all back and then some. Why? Because you have not gotten to the ROOT of what drives you to overeat. Your food is your comfort instead of God. This is satan's stronghold on you.

The Word is the answer to your prayers about your situation not another diet book. How many of you have gone on some of these diets to lose the weight but then fall back into your old ways and ended up gaining it back and then some. Why, because you only did surface work you did not get to the ROOT of what causes you to overeat in the first place. Finding out what the root of the problem is will break the STRONGHOLD of food satan has on you.

Prayer is the most powerful thing you can do, and stay focused, don't let the enemy take your eyes off God. Don't look back look forward.

Your mouth can overcome your mind. Watch your words. Speak God's promises over yourself. Don't let the enemy take God's words from you. FOCUS!

Oh my Strength, I will watch and give heed to You and sing praises; for God is my Defense (my Protector and High Tower).
Psalm 59:9

The battle is within. If I keep my heart at peace it does not matter what spears are thrown at me by the enemy. God will protect me. We fight from the VICTORY thru SURRENDER. You already have it. You just need to receive it and believe it.

One of those spears that fly at us from satan is to distract and make us think about food not God. (Food Spear). Get behind your shield of Faith (Ephesians6).

We need to take our eyes off the challenge that is ahead of us, and especially off of ourselves and put our eyes where they belong on Jesus. We must learn to trust Him, not the diet books. They will do nothing to break your STRONGHOLD of food.

Meditate on these verses and let them drop down in your heart. These are some of the things He tells us in His Word about who we are, and about the power He has given us to live:

*We are crowned with glory and honor (Ps. 8:5)
*We are the light of the world (Matt. 5:14)
*We are more than conquerors through Him who
    Loved us (Romans 8:37)
*We are strengthened with might through His Spirit
    (Eph.3:16)
*He gives us a new heart; one capable of hearing
    and responding to Him (Ezek. 11:19).
*He expects us to share the life He has so generously
    given us and He gives us the power to totally get
    rid of anything that would stand in the way of that
    (Matt. 10:1-8).
*He gives us His authority to do what He asks us to and
    He gives us His protection along with it. (Luke 10:19;
    I John 5:18).
*He supplies ALL our needs (Philippians 4:19).

Rise up and take your place as God's victorious child. Can a diet book do that for you? I don't think so. It is time to stop putting our trust in the things of this world and put that trust in Jesus. He is the one that will give you the power and strength to break that STRONGHOLD of food in your life. He knows us like no one else. He knows our likes and dislikes in food, and he will and can direct us to what He wants us to eat that will help us to be and stay healthy to be able to live the abundant life he wants. If we are giving in to our STRONGHOLD we will not be able to stay healthy and our lives will be much less joyful dealing with illness. I don't know about you but I want to be healthy and strong till the day Jesus comes to get me..Anyone with me?

WRITE ABOUT IT

OK, time to dig. What do you think is the ROOT that drives you to eat for comfort? Really think about this! It is important to look deep within to what you have buried there. It is the road to your FREEDOM..

CHAPTER TEN

Dying to self

When you change your mind you change your life.

We must die to ourselves before we are turned into gentleness, and our crucifixion involves suffering. It will mean experiencing genuine brokenness and a crushing of self, which will be used to affect the heart and conquer the mind. I realize this will be difficult, but please hang in there and let God work to break that STRONGHOLD of food in your life.

The battle for control of our minds is fierce, years of worry rather than trusting God have made us vulnerable to the enemy. Since we now know this, we need to be very vigilant in guarding our minds.

God will use this to draw us closer to Him. We need to ask God to control our minds. I take every thought captive unto the obedience of Christ Jesus, is one of my favorites and I use it a lot. It can keep those Food Spears from hitting you.

What you pay attention too is what you believe, what you believe is what you say and what you say is what you have. Think about what you are saying to yourself. Keep track sometime and see which you have the most of negative or positive statements. You might be surprised. We can say as the leper did to Jesus, "Lord if You will You can make me whole" Matthew 8:2. Also read and study what Proverbs 3:3-4 says. When you think on the positive, the negative cannot get in..

God sends His Spirit to comfort and to strengthen you. All you need to do is ask. God wants to teach you how to comfort yourself without eating food, instead dig into His food.

But I say, walk habitually in the (Holy) Spirit (seek Him and be responsive to His guidance), and then you will certainly not carry out the desire of the sinful nature (Galatians 5:16).

We walk by the Spirit, by setting our affections on Him relying on Him, and seeking to please Him rather than ourselves. You need to rest and trust in Him. As long as you are striving to do the things God is asking of you, such as reading His Word and meditating on it, you will continue to grow and carry out your godly desires rather than your fleshly desires.

God desires for us to change our negative thinking into positive thinking more than we do, because He wants our life to glorify Him. After all we are made in His image..How do you think it would look to always be putting yourself down when you talk to people? Is that how you want to represent God?

"You were taught regarding your previous habit patterns to put off the old person that you were, who is corrupted by deceitful desires, being rejuvenated in the attitude of your mind, and to put on the new person that you are, who is created in God's likeness with righteousness and holiness that come from the truth.
Ephesians 4:22-24
The Christian Counselor's Commentary.

God will enable you to obey Him—remember it's His desire to change you and break that STRONGHOLD of food on you. Change is achieved only through the power of the Holy Spirit. One of the fruits of the Spirit is "self-discipline" which we are after also. Be confident that the Spirit will train you in truth.

"When He, the Spirit of truth comes, He will guide you into all the truth" (John 16:13). He is the one who can teach you how to eat in a way that is pleasing to Him.

It is only as we are taught by the Spirit to put off our old ways and put on our new ones that our thinking about ourselves and food really changes.

The Holy Spirit is the one who convinces, changes and enlightens you. He is the one who will change the way you think about yourself and your eating habits. The Holy Spirit is the only one who knows God's thoughts and he will reveal them to you.

Who among men knows the thoughts of a man except the spirit of the man, which is on him? Even so the thoughts of God no one knows except the Spirit of God. Now we have received, not the spirit of the world, but the Spirit who is from God, that we might know the things freely given to us by God...For who has known the mind of the Lord, that he should instruct Him? But we have the mind of Christ (I Corinthians 2:11-12,16).

Pray for wisdom as you read the passages God directs your too and ask God to send the Holy Spirit to enlighten your understanding so you know what God is telling you personally.

God's Word is powerful, and it is strong enough to strengthen you and to change your thinking about yourself and food. Yes, it is strong enough to break the STRONGHOLD of food or any other STRONGHOLD you may be dealing with.

WRITE ABOUT IT

What do you believe about yourself?

What are you saying about yourself?

If negative thoughts, who helped place these thoughts in your mind growing up?

CHAPTER ELEVEN

Take it back!

We need to regain the territory that satan has stolen from us. We can do this using baby steps if necessary, but we do it by leaning on God's grace and not on ourselves. It is our flesh that tells us to give up, but that is not what God wants. God is looking for people who are ready and willing to do what it takes to break those STRONGHOLDS in our lives. He will be there every step of the way.

> *When you pass through the waters, I will be with you*
> *and through the rivers, this will not overwhelm you.*
> *When you walk through the fire, you will not be burned*
> *Or scorched, nor will the flame kindle up on you.*
> *Isaiah 43:2*

In the rough times is when God is helping us to make spiritual progress. He strengthens and encourages us to keep on going.

It is easy to give up, it takes faith to go through the tough times. When we become bombarded with negative thoughts and we will, then we need to talk back to the devil and tell him, "**I will never give up never!** God is on my side helping me every step of the way. He loves me and VICTORY thru SURRENDER is mine. So I break this STRONGHOLD of food over my life now, in the name of Jesus. You may need to say this several times until your mind and heart connect with it, but that's okay. Strongholds don't happen overnight and sometimes it takes time for our minds to accept our new thinking. You may think this is impossible, NO IT IS NOT! Difficult yes, but God is there with you, growing you every step of the way.

He wants to help you think differently about food. So lean on Him and don't give up!

There is a strong emotional and mental desire that we have for certain foods that we feel bring us comfort in tough times. When we are tired or feeling low we then start to think about that food how good it would taste right then and how much better you would feel. NOT! That is the lie of the devil. You may have a second or two of feeling good, but then here comes the guilt. Is a piece of food worth that? I think not. But satan wants to try and convince you it is. I have fallen into that trap many times until I finally said enough already. This is not what God wants for me or for you. But you have to get to that point where you have had enough of satan's Food Spears.

There are times when God will use guilt to bring us to repentance. If we are going to progress toward change, then we need to look honestly at how we use food in our lives. We must be convinced that when we overeat for whatever excuse we use at the time, that it is gluttony and that is a sin. We need to grasp hold of this truth or we will never hate our sin enough to leave it, and we will keep going down the same path of feeling guilt about our sin.

Maybe you need to ask yourself how much would you like to feel the freedom Jesus died on the cross for? Yes, gluttony is one of the sins He died for. I don't believe we think enough about that one. Well, maybe it is time to look deep within and think about how you feel about what He did for you to be free of the STRONGHOLD of food.

WRITE ABOUT IT.

List those comfort foods you to go. After listing then here if you have them in your home, throw those foods out or give them to the food bank.

List some Bible verses to help strengthen you.

CHAPTER TWELVE

Feeling sorry for ourselves.

One of the biggest things we need to do, is come to the end of ourselves. STOP feeling sorry for ourselves because we can't have some of our favorite foods since they are much too tempting. God is not trying to punish you, he is trying to help you finally live healthier lives. We need His strength, as the Lord said to Paul. "My grace is sufficient for you, for My strength is made perfect in weakness," Paul responded "when I am weak, then I am strong" (2 Corinthians 12:9-10). In this process there will be times when we need God's supernatural grace to break our STRONGHOLDS. We also need to change our thinking about feeling deprived. I mean think about it Deprived of what? Unhealthy foods that make us fat and sluggish and just plain feel awful. Who really wants to feel that way.

DEPRIVE means taking something away from.

Our problem is we have let the world make us think we need to eat all these sugar loaded foods instead of things like fresh fruits and vegetables. We as Christians should be some of the healthiest people around. But, take a look around your church and what do you see? No one wants to talk about being a glutton (glutton=a person who is devoted to eating and drinking to excess) in church. I'm just as guilty. The world has gotten to us more than we would like to admit. I mean do any of you shut off the TV when these mile high burger ads come on? I didn't think so. But, I bet you admit it triggers something in you to want something to munch on that is not a healthy snack. Got ya didn't I..

We are all guilty of this and it just goes to show how strong our STRONGHOLDS are, but the good news is our God is stronger.

Glutton= a person who eats too much.
Gluttony= greediness in eating.

Instead of thinking I feel deprived, think about how good your next doctors report will be because of your new healthy eating habits and the fact you are obeying what God wants you to do to have and sustain good health. You will have more energy and be able to do the things you want and love to do. Wouldn't your family like to have you around for a lot more years? One of my big ones is to no longer dread going to the doctor and getting on that darn scales. Now I look forward to it.

PRAYER:
"God, I confess food is a STRONGHOLD for me. My Stomach has been my God for way too long. I've tried to lose weight too many times on my own and been unsuccessful. Help me Father to get me out of the way, and let you demonstrate your strength through my weakness!

We need to walk in Love not just for others but for ourselves. This is where the Holy Spirit will help you too.

Stop beating up on yourself! We have to learn to be okay with the person God made us to be. Satan counts on us feeling bad about ourselves. He uses that to make your STRONGHOLD even stronger. He uses this by saying things like: no one cares about you, you will always be a failure. So what do you usually do when you hear these things, you run to food instead of God. You allow yourself to get in the way instead of saying Holy Spirit help me! Confess what you need to Him and don't let the devil beat up on you Get yourself out of the way and let the Holy Spirit take over and you will have VICTORY thru SURRENDER.

Loving yourself is not a selfish thing. It is what God wants for you. He wants you to love yourself and see yourself like he does.

Being hooked up to the Holy Spirit is the key to breaking the STRONGHOLD of food or any other Stronghold you may have. Just say Holy Spirit show me how to love myself and to walk in the journey you now have me on.

Working with the Holy Spirit and allowing Him to guide you is what makes you holy and you handle things differently than the world. This is why diets and all those diet books don't work. It doesn't mean the Holy Spirit won't use parts and pieces of some of these books like the Daniel Plan since it is written from a Christian perspective. The Holy Spirit will do what we cannot.

WRITE ABOUT IT.

Write your own prayer for God to give you strength for this journey and thank Him now for your VICTORY thru SURRENDER.

CHAPTER THIRTEEN

Overcomers.

In Jesus we are all OVERCOMERS. In Jesus we can live a disciplined life, our flesh will no longer rule us. Yes, it will be hard at first, but it will become easier as you keep going. Just have God help you to keep your vision of being healthy and strong in front of you.

One of the things I use is what I call a Vision Board. I cut out pictures and positive phrases of things I want to accomplish and put them on a magnetic board or poster board, then I place it somewhere I can see it daily. I use a lot of scripture verses on the board as well. This too helps with changing your mind from negative to positive thoughts about how your see yourself and to put in your mind what you are trying to accomplish. This can help you to get the lasting results you want. We need to be good stewards of the body God has given us it is the only one we get.

It is important also for people who are working on overcoming their STRONGHOLDS of food to avoid people, places, and things that will tempt them. Romans 13:14 says, "But let the Lord Jesus Christ take control of you, and don't think of ways to indulge, or provide for, your evil desires."

It comes down to one question. Just how badly do you want to be free of your STRONGHOLD of food? If you want to give up certain behaviors, then you will need to avoid the people, places, and things that pull you back into your STRONGHOLD. Sometimes change is good and this is one of those times.

As an overcomer, you want to see yourself changed. This is where the vision board helps. It makes your goals more real. It is good to take the pictures from your vision board and mentally see them throughout your day so they become more real to you. Daydreaming about your new life ahead is a good thing. Just grab hold of that new mental picture of who God wants you to be and watch how your eating habits will begin to change.

Then the way you live will always honor and please the Lord, and your lives will produce every kind of good fruit. All the while you will grow as you learn to know God better and better. We also pray that you will be strengthened with all his glorious power so you will have all the endurance and patience you need to share in the inheritance that belongs to his people, who live in the light. For he has rescued us from the kingdom of darkness and transferred us into the Kingdom of his dear Son, who purchased our freedom and forgave our sins. (Colossians1:10-14) (NLT).

God does hear us and He is faithful to be there for us, and He has the power to help us overcome our STRONGHOLDS. All we need to do is cry out to Him on those days we are feeling weak and more like a succumber than an overcomer! Pick up and read the Word. It has a plan for our recovery and it is also the source of power to accomplish it. It provides us the only pathway to wholeness and to overcoming our STRONGHOLD of food.

Everything we need to be overcomers is in God's Word. We can have VICTORY thru SURRENDER and total trust and faith in Him. Keep seeking God and he will lead you in the way that is right for you.

WRITE ABOUT IT.

Make your vision board.

CHAPTER FOURTEEN

Made for more

We were made for a whole lot more than letting our taste buds rule us. We were made to have victory, and living in victory tastes sweeter than any luscious desert you could think of to eat.

We need to be grounded in the truth of who we are in Christ Jesus. This takes studying God's Word and mediating on what he says to you. This will bring you closer to God, and break the STRONGHOLD food has on your life. No more Food Spears coming at you!

Why are we so willing to settle for less than what God has for us? Is it fear of failing again. I realized my failures in this area was because I did not take the time to find out what God had to say about strongholds. I was trying to do this all on my own. The flesh thought she knew better WRONG! This is not something that just changes over night. It takes work and study. It takes time alone with God, and the willingness to listen, trust, and obey.

Faith is confidence in what we hope for and assurance about what we do not see (Hebrews 11:1). Fear is doubt about what we hope for and misgivings about what we do not see.

Fear can be like a leash, leading and pulling you where it wants to go. Fear won't pull you toward success. Fear will disqualify us from so very much of what God has for us. Fear can keep those STRONGHOLDS of food going. Satan loves to use fear. Like I said before you may fall into the fear of failing again. But, we were made for more, we do not have to fail again. VICTORY thru SURRENDER is possible.

Don't let fear hold you back, instead let faith put you on the road to VICTORY thru SURRENDER.

Be not discouraged for God's mercy is new everyday
(La.3:22)

Get into God's ring and rip off the leash of fear and declare who you are. Let God lead you out of being afraid you will fail again into being sure you will succeed. He can lead you from fearful to faithful, allow Him to awake your heart to all the blessings he has for you by surrendering your STRONGHOLD of food to Him.

What is holding you back from being more? What is keeping you stuck? Sadly many of us are unable to open the treasures of God's goodness.

I pray that the eyes of your heart may be enlightened in order that *you may know the hope to which he has called you, the riches of his glorious inheritance in his holy people*
(Eph.1:8)

Grab unto faith and hope. What you pursue will determine your breakthrough. Hold unto the truth he declares about you.

I do believe, help me overcome my unbelief! (Mark 9:24)

You will show me the path of life; in your presence is fullness of joy, at your right hand there are pleasures forevermore
Psalm 16:11

We need to dwell on God's Promises. What God has given to you is enough to improve you.

> *Through these he has given us his very great precious promises, so that through them you may participate in the divine nature, having escaped the corruption in the world caused by evil desires.*
> *2Peter 1:4*

Stand on God's Word! Hold on to the truths he declares about you. He too says you were made for more. Just open yourself to the fullness of God's spiritual riches for you.

WRITE ABOUT IT

Take some time with God right now and write about what he is speaking to your heart.

CHAPTER FIFTEEN

Disciplined commitment

It is important to have a hope and power beyond ourselves to allow God to break the STRONGHOLD of food. He is the only one with the power to do this. Do not think for a minute you can be successful without him. Just ask yourself, "Self how successful were you in the past?" Without his help those old feelings of failure, discouragement, and defeat will come rushing back into your thoughts. This is not what we want our mind and hearts to be filled with. We want to be filled with hope, truth, and power. The power that raised Christ from the dead is also available to us as born again believers.

It is up to us to decide if we want to continue on the vicious cycle of making excuses for ourselves like choosing food over God, or do we want to finally taste success and allow God to break that STRONGHOLD of food that satan has had over you for so long. It is up to you to stay on the path of hard work and perseverance because it will take both of these to be successful and to embrace your true identity which is in God not food. God wants us to operate in the hope and power that is nothing like we have ever experienced. He loves us so much and he does not want to see us all bound up in the STRONGHOLD of food.

So start now to position your heart toward God and allow him to break those food STRONGHOLDS in your life or for that matter any other stronghold you may have.

So since you have been reading scripture while reading this book, in view of these scriptures what are your thoughts about how you feel about food? Have you been able to come up with new ideas to make the changes necessary to break your STRONGHOLDS of food? I believe God is showing you ways to make the changes necessary because He knows you want to eat in a way that glorifies Him. This means doing away with any sinful habits.

Stop now and think about any sinful habit you may be hanging onto that is keeping your STRONGHOLD of food going. If you can establish a bad habit, guess what you can also develop and commit to godly habits because the power of all of heaven is on your side.

With the power of the Holy Spirit we can make that commitment to change our old sinful habits

> *Do not let sin reign in your mortal body that you should obey*
> *Its lusts, and do not go on presenting the members of your*
> *body to sin as instruments of unrighteousness; but*
> *present yourselves to God as those alive from the dead,*
> *and your members as instruments of righteousness to God*
> *Romans 6:12-13*

You might think what if my STRONGHOLD of food is too strong? I've tried so many times to change and I keep falling back into my old sin. Paul's answer to this is in Romans 6:14, "Sin shall not be master over you, for you are not under law, but under grace."

This is why it is so important to make that disciplined commitment to God and studying His Word, because if it was up to our flesh we would keep failing, but the good news is we have God's strengthening power!

When you feel tempted to reach for more food than you need say, "Sin will not master over me." You can have VICTORY thru SURRENDER by committing yourself to God, it gives you the determination not to give the enemy any weapons to use against you.

Continue to declare, "Sin will not be master over me." Say this with faith and the assurance that this is God's will for you.

WRITE ABOUT IT.

Think about the excuses you use for yourself.

CHAPTER SIXTEEN

Growing closer to God

You may be asking yourself, "How do I grow closer to God?" Well, one way is by making the choice to deny yourself something that is permissible but not beneficial. Say for instance that chocolate brownie you love to have. It is permissible to have it, but you need to ask is this brownie beneficial to me. All food is permissible but not all is beneficial to our health. In Luke 9:23 Jesus said, 'If anyone would come after me, he must deny himself and take up his cross daily and follow me.

I want to become a woman of self-discipline which honors God and helps me to live a life of self-control which happens to be one of the fruits of the Spirit (Galatians 5:22).

I would rather feel closer to Jesus and what he wants for me each day as opposed to feeling guilty about the poor choices my flesh wants to make.

Satan holds food in front of us and will say things like 'You will never win the battle you have with food. You have failed in the past and you will fail again, so you might as well just give in and eat what you want. Satan wants to draw our hearts into a place for us to be defeated. He does not want your STRONGHOLD broken. But, the Word says in Romans 8:1, "and if the Spirit of him who raised Christ from the dead will also give life to your mortal bodies through his Spirit, who lives in you." The Spirit living within us is what gives us the power to change our thinking towards food and resist any temptation the devil may decide to throw at us.

Paul says in Galatians 5:25, "since we live by the Spirit, let us keep in step with the Spirit." In other words, as we read and study God's Word we need to ask the Holy Spirit to teach us how to put what we have read into practice in our lives.

> *For, as I have told you before and now say again even with tears, many live as enemies of the cross of Christ. Their destiny is destruction, their god is their stomach, and their glory is in their shame. Their mind is on earthly things.*
> *Philippians 3:18-19*

As you can see in the verse above Paul is telling us that food can become so consuming that people find themselves ruled by the food rather than God. That is what we call a STRONGHOLD of FOOD.

Daily pray the scriptures relating to your struggle until you experience freedom. Here are a few you can use:

> *But He replied, It has been written, Man shall not live and be upheld and sustained by bread alone, but by every word that comes forth from the mouth of God.*
> *Matthew 4:4, AMP*

> *Therefore I tell you, stop being perpetually uneasy (anxious and worried) about your life, what you shall eat or what you shall drink; or about your body, what you shall put on. Is not life greater (in quality) than food, and the body (far above and more excellent) than clothing?*
> *Matthew 6:25*

> *Keep awake and watch and pray (constantly), that you may not enter into temptation; the spirit indeed is willing, but*

the flesh is weak.
Mark 14:38

Man shall not live and be sustained by (on) bread alone but by every word and expression of God.
Luke 4:4

Jesus replied, I am the Bread of Life. He who comes to Me will never be hungry and he who believes in and cleaves to and trusts in and relies on Me will never thirst anymore (at any time).
John 6:35

Clothe yourself with the Lord Jesus (the Messiah), and make no provision for (indulging) the flesh (put a stop to thinking about the evil cravings of your physical nature) to (gratify its) desires (lusts).
Romans 13:14

So that he can no longer spend the rest of his natural life living by (his) human appetites and desires, but (he lives) for what God wills.
1 Peter 4:2

Little children keep yourselves from idols (false gods)- (from anything and everything that would occupy the place in your heart due to God, from any sort of substitute for Him that would take first place in your life).
1 John 5:21

    As you grow closer to God, He will teach you His ways and give you His strength. It is important for us to spend time in prayer on a daily basis. It doesn't need to be long prayers, some days I can only say "Jesus help!" We need our food daily to keep our bodies healthy, well we also need daily prayer to keep our spirit fed, for growth to occur in our walk with Jesus. I've had people tell me they don't know how to talk to God. Talk to Him just like you would a friend. After all He is your best friend.

The Bible says that we are to "live a life worthy of the calling you have received. Be completely humble and gentle; be patient, bearing with one another in love" Ephesians 4:1-3. God wants us to grow in our "knowledge of the Son of God and become mature, attaining to the whole measure of the fullness of Christ" Ephesians 4:13.

Christians want to live lives close to God, this is why we read and study His Word it helps us to learn about Him and His love for us.

> *"Instead you thrill to God's Word, you chew on Scripture day and night. You're a tree replanted in Eden, bearing fresh fruit every month, never dropping a leaf, always in blossom.*
> *Psalm 1:2-3, The Message*

The Bible provides access to God's thoughts and commands on practically every topic of life. As we read His Word, this draws us closer and closer to Him and we begin to learn how to live life a different way.

When we come to know and love His views, it will cause us to change some of the bad habits we have been hanging onto and once again we will continually grow closer to God.

WRITE ABOUT IT.

What are some things you plan to do to grow closer to God?

CHAPTER SEVENTEEN

Turn it over.

Ever since I started writing this book, there has been a battle raging with satan. You see, I am on this journey of breaking the STRONGHOLD of food just like you are. Believe me when you have had strongholds in your life for quite sometime satan does not want them broken. Every day is a day for me to have VICTORY thru SURRENDER. Every day I surrender more to Him.

The last few days have been tough for me. Have you ever had times when you want to just eat, but you did not know why? You aren't hungry but something says EAT something and you will feel better. I had that going on, and I hate to say I gave into it. Did I feel better? I think you know the answer to that one. NO! I just wanted something else, when what I just ate did not satisfy me. I can see you out there shaking your head yes and saying I know what you mean. We are looking for comfort from food at that time rather than God.

One of the worst things that comes from this is the guilt you feel afterwards, and it is like satan is there whispering in your ear "I won." Then I feel like I let God down. Actually I let myself down. Here I am writing this book about defeating strongholds and I'm still working on breaking mine. But I do feel it necessary to be honest. So when I say I know how you feel I mean it. But, God said I will be tested so that I can tell you that VICTORY comes thru SURRENDER to Him. He also reminded me that there are days when I am still trying to fight this battle on my own, so he has to remind me I cannot fight satan, nor do I need to. I just need to turn it over to him and let him fight my battle.

Pray scripture as a preventive measure as well as a protective measure. But, don't just pray the scriptures that is not enough, you must also apply the truth of the scriptures to your life. Scripture contains the abundance of true life in Jesus, that we need to act upon, accept, be grateful for, and trust to change our lives. We need also to change our thoughts and work on those emotions we ladies seem to have. I think you know what I'm talking about.

Our behavior springs out of our thoughts and our emotions. Our thoughts and emotions do affect our eating habits. I know when I am emotionally upset, I will go looking for comfort food to feel better. Anybody relate!

The Bible tells us we need to discipline our thoughts. We need to become conformed to God's thinking in every area of our lives, and especially in the area of our eating habits.

In Philippians 4:8, Paul tells us how we are to govern our thoughts: For the rest, brethren, whatever is true, whatever is worthy of reverence and is honorable and seemly, whatever is just, whatever is pure, whatever is lovely and lovable, whatever is kind and winsome and gracious, if there is any virtue and excellence, if there is anything worthy of praise, think on and weigh and take account of these things (fix your minds on them).

We need to identify our sinful thoughts that lead to our sinful actions and then encourage ourselves to think on godly thoughts that will lead to godly actions. As we practice doing this, we will find it becomes easier to take our thoughts captive and we become aware quicker of the negative thoughts that satan is trying to put in our minds in order to sabotage the changes we are making.

God is on our side! He wants us to break the STRONGHOLD of food on our lives as much as we want. Don't get discouraged if you get off track along the way. This is the process that Paul wrote about in 2 Corinthians 10:5: "We are destroying speculations and ever lofty thing raised up against the knowledge of God, and we are taking every thought captive to the obedience of Christ Jesus."

Remember Jesus was also tempted by satan but He answered satan in this way: "Man shall not live on bread alone, but on every word that proceeds out of the mouth of God." (Matthew 4:4). Your growth as well as trusting God enough to turn it over to Him is dependent upon your consuming God's Word. All you need to do is begin right now. Let your comfort come from Him not food. Let Him be first in your life and allow Him to control your thoughts and your actions.

WRITE ABOUT IT

Have you turned your battle over to God yet? Or, are you still trying to do it yourself?

CHAPTER EIGHTEEN

Where is the trust.

I have asked myself why is this so hard to do? It is a simple thing to just lay it down at the cross, but then why do I feel I still need to get my flesh involved? I think it partly has to do with TRUST. We need to ask ourselves, "self, do I trust God enough to let him do this for me?" Or maybe I need to ask do I feel deserving to have Him fight this battle? All the years of weighing more than I know I should, going on every diet out there with short lived success, why do I find it so hard to give it over to God? Sometimes it is also necessary in this process to do some real soul searching.

This is one of those areas when I feel we have allowed the world to get into our minds and hearts too much. I mean how many healthy ads do you see on TV, over the double or triple sized burgers? How many fruit or vegetables commercials do you see. We get bombarded with ads telling us to eat unhealthy foods on a daily basis. Then the next thing you will see is an ad about taking some new medication to prevent heart attacks and strokes, REALLY! We all know that a better and cheaper way is to eat food God wants us to eat. It is so simple but we make it so difficult for ourselves.

We know when we are about to eat something we shouldn't. I always feel this deep down tug that is saying "don't eat that", but do I always obey it. No! How about you? Be honest with yourself now.

I am working hard to change my eating habits and I and God have done pretty well. I still have areas to work on, but I am in such a different place than I was say even a year ago. I have learned to work on one thing at a time. God knows that I can get overwhelmed if I don't do it just right. This is when I start with the negative talk if I have gotten off track. He has been teaching me to be patient with myself. We can be so patient with other people but put ourselves on a very short leash. I have been noticing that at one time I use to live to eat now I eat to live. I am making healthier choices. Yes, I still have those break down days, but I am learning that is okay, I just pick myself up, and allow God to show me what was going on somewhere in my mind to drive me there. If I just ask God and that goes for all of us he will show us. I think sometimes we are afraid to ask because it will mean looking within to fix something that is out of whack. I am finding that the more I ask God to help me, the better I am feeling.

Victory over this STRONGHOLD doesn't always come immediately, there are things that God wants us to confront and then lay it down at the cross, this way satan can never use it against us again. With each obedient step I take by surrendering to God, helps me to know I have the VICTORY thru SURRENDER.

> *"You shall keep my statues and practice them; I am the Lord who sanctifies (changes) you."*
> *Leviticus 20:8*

This journey won't be over in a short period of time. The journey we are on to godliness takes a lifetime, but don't fret, He will be with you all the way giving you the encouragement you need to keep moving forward.

This has become such a world of instant gratification that we don't want to wait for anything, but sometimes God needs this time to make the changes that He desires in you. Sometimes He is just trying to get you to rely totally on Him. This is why we need to fight against discouragement and keep moving forward. Change is possible only with Him, so we need to cooperate with Him. Real change requires adjustments in our attitude and our minds. This takes time and total reliance on God to get the desired results that we want.

WRITE ABOUT IT

Do you trust God to help you do this? Why or why not.

CHAPTER NINETEEN

Trust and believe

Every sin action is a reaction to our unbelief. God wants to break those STRONGHOLDS on our lives, but we need to TRUST and BELIEVE he will. You ever notice how easy it is to do this for other people, but how hard it is to do for ourselves. Why do you think that is?

     For myself, I think I do not believe I deserve the best. Others do, but not me! Why? Because I never had earthly parents who gave me support growing up. Everything was negative. In other words curses were spoken over me. When negative words are spoken over you for years and then you meet challenges in life as an adult, you will once again hear the words you heard as a child. Words like, fatty, you will never amount to anything, you can't do anything right and on and on. We get snared by our thoughts and words that come out of our own mouth on bad days. Do you ever tell yourself I'm such a failure, I cannot do this, maybe you can't but God can! It is time to change the way we think and speak about ourselves. The negative is what the devil uses to bring you down.

     God loves us so much, and it hurts him to hear us speak in such negative ways about ourselves. He does not want us to be so bound up and unhappy. He wants to set you free. You just need to believe he does and then allow him to do His work in you.

     Talk to yourself, talk to that wounded little child that lives within you and change your thinking to God's way of thinking about you. You are the righteousness of God and you deserve to live a life free from STRONGHOLDS that hold you back from living <u>the kind</u>

of life God wants you to live. You are a beautiful, strong, intelligent child of God. Now say those words to yourself everyday and believe them because they are true.

One thing to remember when we are giving into that STRONGHOLD of food, we are feeding or stuffing God's home. This is one part I believe we want to try and forget about as we are stuffing our faces. At these times we are not thinking about God and what he wants, we are indulging the devil and what he wants. Sobering thought isn't it.

> *"If we confess our sins, He is faithful and righteous to forgive us our sins and to cleanse us from all unrighteousness.*
> *(I John 1:9)*

One of the things we can do to fight back against the devil is to have a thankful heart toward God. Satan hates that because it will begin to lift you up against unbelief .Psalms is a great place to go in the Bible for this. Here are a few to get you started:

> *You have turned my mourning into dancing for me;*
> *you have taken off my sackcloth and clothed me with joy,*
> *That my soul may sing praise to you and not be silent.*
> *O Lord my God, I will give thanks to your forever.*
> *Psalm 30:11-12*

> *I will give thanks and praise You, O Lord my God, with all my heart; and will glorify your name forevermore. For great is Your lovingkindness and graciousness toward me; and You have rescued my life from the depths of Sheol (from death).*
> *Psalm 86:12-13*

The righteous will flourish like the date palm (long-lived upright and useful);
they will grow like a cedar in Lebanon (majestic and stable)
Psalm 92:12

Allow God to help you find the time to be able to praise Him for every small victory cause they count too.

Also remember to make time for prayer. All this He loves and He will draw you nearer to Him. Taking time to read your Bible is so important. We need to feast on His Words not just on bread alone. God wants us to hide His Word in our hearts, so when the devil tries to tempt us we will kick his tail by repeating God's Word. Reading and studying His Word will also help you to make progress in changing your thinking. Consider this an exercise for your brain that will benefit you like physical exercise does for your body or maybe more so.

WRITE ABOUT IT

What were the negative words spoken over you? Write them down, then tell satan "I am the righteousness of God and tear that sheet up and throw those words out of your life. Replace with God's Word about you...

Write the scripture that God speaks to your heart about how he feels about you...

CHAPTER TWENTY

Fear.

I talked earlier about how easy it is to see others successful, but not ourselves. This comes from negative words that were spoken to us in childhood. Along with that comes fear. The number one fear is that what God has promised in His Word will not come to pass in our life. This is the number one fear satan wants us to have. This fear has made many of us give up too soon instead of pressing forward.

Unbelief and fear go hand in hand. In your mind you are thinking I'm afraid I will fail again and you never challenge who you could be.

When God wants to accomplish something in your life, satan will do everything he can to prevent it from happening. Let yourself become a reservoir of the Spirit's fruits, this will fill you more than all the worldly food you crave.

Sin (gluttony) impacts the relationships you are in. Being overweight and so tied to food, affects how we feel about ourselves. Satan uses this to beat us down and it hurts our self-esteem and confidence in most everything we do.

God wants us to believe in Him and he will take care of the things that trouble us. We need to get rid of some old thinking (I can't stress this enough) and replace it with God's thinking. We are not meant to be in bondage to anything. We are meant to have VICTORY thru SURRENDER!

Why spend money on what is not bread,

and your labor on what does not satisfy?
Listen, listen to me, and eat what is good,
and eat what is good, and you will delight in
the richest of fare.
                Isaiah 55:2

Instead of the food we are tempted with that makes our bodies fat, eat the food of the Bible and let your soul get fat.

God is asking you why do you fear? Why do you sin by not trusting in me to bring the victory into your life you so desire? He has promised to defeat every demonic power that comes against you. So if He promises this then we need to ask why are we so fearful of letting God pull down that STRONGHOLD of food?!

"Lay aside every weight, and the sin which so easily ensnares us" (Hebrews 12:1)

Victory comes when we pray in faith and expect and believe God to answer our prayer. Our problem is not the absence of faith but rather unbelief. You need to consider the Promise not the problem. The battle is won in your mind. Unbelief comes in through our thought process. Change your thoughts, change your life!

Satan wants to make you think and believe that God will not keep His promises to us. Fear comes through unbelief. Faith is believing God will.

The (reverent) fears of the Lord (that is, worshiping Him and regarding His as truly awesome) is the beginning and the preeminent part of knowledge (its starting point and its essence); But arrogant fools despise (skillful and godly) wisdom and instruction and self-discipline.
                                      Proverbs 1:7

*Your word I have treasured and stored in my heart,
that I may not sin against You.*
Psalm 119:11

*Why are you in despair, O my soul?
And why have you become restless
and disturbed within me?
Hope in God and wait expectantly
for Him, for I shall again praise Him
for the help of His presence.*
Psalm 42:5

The mind is the arena of faith. Everything comes from our thinking. You can't ignore what you are thinking about, but you can have authority over what you think. If you are always thinking on the negative that works the same as if you are thinking in the positive. So you need to take the authority God has given you over negative thoughts and put and keep your thoughts on God and His promises.

So find a promise in God's Word that speaks to you and then work with it. Write it in your journal let God use it to speak to your heart.

WRITE ABOUT IT

What are your fears?

CHAPTER TWENTY-ONE

John 10:10

> *The thief comes only in order to steal and destroy.*
> *I came that they may have and enjoy life, and have*
> *it in abundance (to the full, till it overflows).*
> John 10:10

As you can see from the verse above satan wants to destroy us and one of the ways he does this is by creating STRONGHOLDS in our lives. Then as you read on you see what Jesus wants for our lives, He wants us to enjoy our life and have life in abundance. Jesus does not want us to be bound up by STRONGHOLDS.

> *He personally bore our sins in His (own) body on the*
> *tree (as on an altar and offered Himself on it), that we*
> *might die (cease to exist) to sin and live to righteousness.*
> *By His wounds you have been healed.*
> *1Peter 2:24*

We keep filling ourselves with empty calories instead of the food of God's Word which will fill you up so full that the devil cannot tempt you with whatever the food is you are craving.

As I write this book, the devil has been pounding on me. Just now, I just finished my breakfast and I'm not hungry but satan is trying to convince me that I need some comfort food. Ever have that happen? Think about the times when you started reading the Bible, doing a Bible study or just reading a book you knew God wanted you to read, when suddenly the thought comes to you "gosh, I think I want a snack to go with this reading." Do you think that was God?

I don't think so, because you were already snacking on God's food for your life. The devil is sneaky and his play ground is our minds.

When the apostle Paul says, "their god is their stomach," he means that food can become so consuming that people find themselves ruled by it, in other words it has become a STRONGHOLD. If we allow the devil to keep us bound up in this STRONGHOLD, it will begin to affect our relationship with God. We will begin to feel increasingly distant from Him, because we know we are being disobedient and we are giving into the devil.

We need to rejoice in everything God asks us to do, because it will always result in blessings. We need to also learn what pleases Him. He tells you in His Word. One of the reasons it is so important to study your Bible on a regular basis. As we study Him, he will pour His life into us.

Think on these promises as you go forward pleasing Him:

"So you shall keep My statues and My judgments, by which, if a person keeps them, he shall live;
I am the Lord"
Leviticus 18:5

I call heaven and earth as witnesses against you today, that I have set before you life and death, the blessing and the curse; therefore, you shall choose life in order that you may live, you and your descendants, by loving the Lord your God, by obeying His voice, and by holding closely to Him; for He is your life (your good life, your abundant life, your fulfillment) and the length of your days, that you may live in the land which the Lord promised (swore) to give your fathers, to Abraham, Isaac, and Jacob.
Deut. 30:19-20

God is so good. He promises to protect us from the devils sneaky little tricks. We just need to trust, believe and obey. He offers us life, blessings, peace, and much more when we seek to please Him.

WRITE ABOUT IT

How do you feel when you end up giving into your flesh and eat something you know you don't need?

Does it make you feel distant from God?

CHAPTER TWENTY-TWO

How

How do STRONGHOLDS get started? A stronghold is usually something you run to. It is a form of protection so your mind tells you another lie of satan because it can also snare you. It imprisons you as it protects you. This is a false protection.

When life gets tough, we go back to what is familiar to us. God wants us to cast our burden on Him (see Psalm 55:22). He wants us to trust in, lean on, and confidently rely on Him. He did not say to rely on food now did he? As it states in 1Peter 5:7;

> *Casting the whole of your care (all your anxieties, all your concerns, once and for all) on Him, for He cares for you affectionately and cares about you watchfully.*

You notice it says ALL not just some, ALL!

Let's talk a little about obedience and disobedience and discipline. Why does the word discipline scare us so much? Why do we rebel so strongly against it when we know it is for our own good. God doesn't just say; Oh you have been such a bad girl today Pauline, I need to discipline you. No, he does it because he knows He loves us so much he only wants us to live in good health.

Obedience will not remove the obstacles, but it will help us to navigate through them. Obedience compels us to live by trust not by results and rewards.

"For the time being no discipline brings joy,

but seems grievous and painful; but afterwards it yields a peaceable fruit of righteousness to those who have been trained by it."(Hebrews 12:11)

A life of discipline begins with a disciplined mind. Here we are again "change your thoughts, change your life." We need to stay focused on our desires and goals and a disciplined mind will do just that and it will also help you to be more productive. A disciplined mind keeps you thinking on positive thoughts which give you energy and help you feel happy about what you have been able to accomplish regardless of how large or small that accomplishment might be. Negative thoughts do nothing but pull you down. So if you are tempted to think negative thoughts, just take that thought captive and release it to God. Then speak His Words to yourself.

Discipline is not a bad thing. It is what will finally set us free from those STRONGHOLDS of food or any stronghold we may have.

I have seen in my own life the more disciplined I become the less I think about food. I have started to ask myself am I really hungry? If not I don't eat. This is such a great feeling! When I still was battling with my STRONGHOLD of food I would just eat hungry or not. This has all just recently started to change. The closer I grow to Jesus, the stronger I am getting. This is an accomplishment to celebrate!

Another big thing in this healing process is to RECEIVE our healing. We pray about it but sometimes we forget to say I RECEIVE my healing. Jesus thank you for breaking this STRONGHOLD off of me.

Align your thinking with God's truth and you will begin to feel stronger and you will have a deeper desire to be obedient to Him. This requires time and effort on your part, but don't give up and He will bless you and the efforts you are making to accomplish your goal. You will have VICTORY thru SURRENDER.

"For the time being no discipline brings joy, but seems grievous and painful; but afterwards it yields a peaceable fruit of righteousness to those who have been trained by it."
Hebrews 12:11

WRITE ABOUT IT

When life gets tough what is it that you run back to that is familiar and comforting to you?

If a certain food, are you ready to give it up?

CHAPTER TWENTY-THREE

Holy Spirit

Have you ever had the experience of the Holy Spirit nudging you in connection with your food choices? If so what did you do, obey or ignore Him? Do you have certain foods that you find almost impossible to walk away from? Well guess what, that is an indication you have a STRONGHOLD with that food.

These are probably what you consider comfort foods. What thoughts and feelings arise when you think about giving these foods up? Probably a bit of P-A-N-I-C. Satan wants you to believe that food comforts you more than God's food. But, the devil's food only lasts tell the last bite. God's food stored up in our hearts lasts forever, and it will power us to VICTORY thru SURRENDER.

In Dr. Caroline Leaf's book, Who Switched off My Brain, she writes; a log of research is available on how food affects your mood. Scientists at the Massachusetts Institute of Technology were among the first to document this. Many others including researcher's at Harvard Medical School, have followed suit. For example, scientists call carbohydrates-found in pasta, breads and sweets- "comfort foods" because they boost the powerful brain chemical, serotonin which is involved in feelings of contentment. But the comfort won't last long. Within twenty minutes of eating processed carbohydrates, any benefits will dissipate.

If we dedicate this journey of breaking the STRONGHOLD of food to God, he promises the Holy Spirit will guide you every step of the way. With the Holy Spirit, we have more power than we could ever think of having on our own.

The greatest satisfaction we can seek is the satisfaction of being obedient to God. Our bodies are a gift from God and sometime I think we forget that fact. We need to be faithful and take care of this gift. After all it is the temple that the Holy Spirit lives in.

> *But the Helper (Comforter, Advocate, Intercessor-Counselor, Strengthener, Standby), the Holy Spirit, Whom the Father will send in my name (in my place, to represent Me and act on My behalf), He will teach you all things. And He will help you remember everything that I have told you.*
> *John 14:26*

We need to recognize that the Spirit does not equal power, but that where the Spirit of God is there is power. Ask God to meet you with His love, and let the Holy Spirit open up your past hurts and bring healing. This is so important to do. There are many of you out there who have not let go of past hurts and this can keep you locked to the STRONGHOLD of food. The devil uses our pain to have us run to food to stuff the pain back down, but it will just come back up again. Until we confront the pain and allow God to have it once and for all.

We can continually be filled with His Presence. It once again all has to do with our thinking. Ask yourself what am I thinking about? Now more than ever we need to have the power of God working in our lives. Like Psalm 150 says, "Let everything that has breath praise the Lord. Praise the Lord!"

> *Do you not know and understand that you (the church) are the temple of God, and that the Spirit of God dwells (permanently) in you (collectively and individually)*
> *I Corinthians 3:16*

Do you not know that your body is a temple of the Holy Spirit who is within you, whom you have (received as a gift) from God, and that you are not your own (property)?
I Corinthians 6:19

Start praising Him now! He is going to give you the strength you need to give up those comfort foods that are keeping you in bondage.

WRITE ABOUT IT.

Do you feel panic as you think about giving up your comfort food?

What will you replace your comfort food with?

CHAPTER TWENTY-FOUR

Greatest days

Your greatest days are ahead of you not behind you.

We need to take our eyes off of the challenge that is ahead of us, off food and off ourselves. Instead we need to put our eyes on Jesus and His Word.

Ask yourself how often in a day's time do you think about food? Probably more than you realize. Wonder what would happen in your life if all those thoughts were about God and His Word hummmm, I think, no I know something would most certainly change.

I also need to do what I need to, to break the STRONGHOLD food has had on me for so many years. I need to be all in with Jesus, and allow Him to take me to the next level. Whatever you give yourself to will give back. Give yourself to Jesus and let him free you from the STRONGHOLD of food.

We are more than conquerors through Him who loved us.
Romans 8:37

Satan will come against you hard because he does not want you to have VICTORY, because then you will also be able to help others who struggle with this. Satan wants to destroy us before we know the truth of what he is doing to us. God did not say this would be easy and that we would not have challenges, but He did promise that he will be with us and that he "will never leave us nor forsake us."

(Hebrews 13:5). We can most certainly be victorious, because of Jesus!

> I love Romans 8:11;
> *But if the Spirit of Him who raised Jesus from the dead dwells in you, He who raised Christ from the dead will also give life to your mortal bodies through His Spirit who dwells in you.*

The same Holy Spirit that raised Jesus from the dead is in you as well. We have the power as children of God to live in the abundance of life he has for us. He does not want you to be bound up, he wants you to be free to enjoy all he has blessed you with. I encourage you to rise up and take authority over satan that you have been given as a child of God.

> *I am God's child, for I am born-again of the incorruptible seed of "the Word of God which lives and abides forever."*
> *1Peter 1:23*

The spiritual weapons are available to each of us, but we need to take hold of them and use them. When we take hold of the weapons God has given us, we will have VICTORY! So take God's Word and speak it out, fight that old devil do not give in or give up. When it gets hard, you have been given authority over the devil (see Luke 9:1) so USE IT!

WRITE ABOUT IT

When your mind starts to drift to food what are you going to do?

Write some scriptures about temptation.

CHAPTER TWENTY-FIVE

Surrender first step

> *So if the Son liberates you (makes you free), then you are really and unquestionably free.*
> *John 8:36*

Also read Romans 8:1. Even when we fall off the wagon, there is no condemnation for us. So if God doesn't condemn me then I do not need to beat myself up either. I just need to pick myself up, thank Him for loving me even when I give into my temptations and then move on to what I know he is asking me to do to get my eating in order.

When temptation hits pay attention to what you are feeling and thinking. Take time to get quiet and listen. When you hear the alarm go off inside as you are getting ready to eat that tempting food, walk away, it is God talking to you. God is too much of a gentleman to force you to walk away. It is up to you to listen and obey.

The presence of God is a place to go to process your emotions. Sometimes what you run to will ruin you. Temptation is not a sin. It is when we ACT on that temptation that it becomes sin. Like giving into that comfort food when you know God is saying NO.

The devil cannot defeat someone who refuses to give up. You have authority in the name of Jesus as I pointed out earlier and like I said then USE IT! Talk to your problem about what Jesus has already done.

Meditate on His promises everyday. You need to meditate in the Word until you can see yourself doing it. Cover your situation in the Word. Promises like the following in Joshua 1:8-9

> *This Book of the Law shall not depart out of your mouth, but you shall meditate on it day and night, that you may observe and do according to all that is written in it. For then you shall make your way prosperous, and then you shall deal wisely and have good success.*
> *Have not I commanded you? Be strong, vigorous, and very courageous. Be not afraid, neither be dismayed, for the Lord your God is with you where-ever you go.*

Also study and meditate on Proverbs 4:20-24.

We are the only ones who can keep ourselves from receiving God's good for us. He does not want to keep those things from us. The devil can't keep those things from us either only we can do that!

Our minds are not instantly changed at the moment of our new birth. If our minds are full of stronghold thinking, truth can be twisted if it is filtered through this kind of thinking.

The good news is Jesus has given to us the keys we need to deal with all of our strongholds and our mental traps. He has given us supernatural, powerful, keys like the following;

> *I will give you the keys of the kingdom of heaven; and whatever you bind (declare to be improper and unlawful) on earth must be what is already bound in heaven; and whatever you loose (declare lawful) on earth must be what is already loosed in heaven.*
> *Matthew 16:19*

> *Truly I tell you, whatever you forbid and declare to be*

Improper and unlawful on earth must be what is already forbidden in heaven, and whatever you permit and declare proper and lawful on earth must be what is already permitted in heaven.
Matthew 18:18

If you just read the Bible for several hours a day, but then you just close it up and walk away this won't help you with your STRONGHOLDS of food. But if you will stop and meditate on what you have just read and allow God to speak to your heart, and you act upon and accept, and are thankful for and trust His Words, this is what will begin to change your thinking and your life. God is our partner in this journey. We do not need to go it alone.

We are assured and know that (God being a partner in their labor) all things work together and are (fitting into a plan) for good to and for those who love God and are called according to (His) design and purpose.
Romans 8:28

WRITE ABOUT IT.

What emotion do you struggle with that can cause the devil to tempt you with food.

CHAPTER TWENTY-SIX

Power

Power is the ability to get the job done.

You need to be educated in the Word of God to know when satan is lying to you. He can be very sly in the way he lies. Don't even crack the door a bit cause that is all he needs to get in. Bind him up and cover yourself in the Blood of Jesus

We also can learn a lot about ourselves by just listening to the words we are speaking to ourselves. Try taping yourself for a day and just see if more positive or negative words come out of that mouth. It can be very revealing as to why we have the STRONGHOLD of food on our lives.

You need to get in agreement with what God's Word says about you. If you have been down on yourself for a long time, it will feel unnatural to say these words about you. But give it time and let God work then suddenly you will see who you truly are and believe who you truly are in God's eyes. The Word of God in our mouth has POWER to destroy the STRONGHOLD of food.

Isaiah 55:10-11 reads:
For as the rain and snow come down from the heavens,
and return not there again, but water the earth and make
it bring forth and sprout, that it may give seed to the sower
and bread to the eater,
So shall My Word be that goes forth out of My mouth:
it shall not return to Me void (without producing any
effect, useless), but it shall accomplish that which I

please and purpose, and it shall prosper in the thing for which I sent it.

What you water in your thinking will grow. God invites us to think on his level. Like it reads in Colossians 3:1-2;

If then you have been raised with Christ (to a new life, thus sharing His resurrection from the dead), aim at and seek the (rich, eternal treasures) that are above, where Christ is, seated at the right hand of God.

And set your minds and keep them set on what is above (the highest things), not on the things that are on the earth.

We need to learn to seek all of God's truth for our situation and then act upon it with complete surrender to make the right choices. One of our biggest problems is the vulnerability of our damaged souls and the defenses your soul has erected in order to try and protect you.

When you have stronghold thinking, you are opening yourself up to attacks from the devil. This kind of thinking moves you out from under God's protection.

The word loose in Matthew 16:19 means to destroy any wrong thinking in your mind. God has promised restoration all through His word.

But be transformed (changed) by the (entire) renewal of your mind (by its new ideals and its new attitude) so that you may prove (for yourselves) what is the good and acceptable and perfect will of God.
Romans 12:2

As believers, we can all walk in the power of the Holy Spirit, receive from God and we can then receive our deliverance. It's called VICTORY thru SURRENDER.

WRITE ABOUT IT

Get in a quiet place and think about how you are feeling about yourself. Write about your feelings. This can be difficult but very revealing. It is also the road to healing, releasing all the bad feelings that you have about yourself. They are just lies of the devil.

CHAPTER TWENTY-SEVEN

Talk to yourself

We need to ask ourselves on a daily basis, "am I going to live by the flesh or the Spirit today?"

We are a spirit, a soul, and a body, and what happens in our spirit and soul affects our bodies. God gave us emotions, but he did not intend for those emotions to rule our lives. Satan uses these emotions to rule our lives. Satan uses these emotions to get us to fill up on earthly food rather than God's food. When we sense this temptation coming on, we need to RUN to God and His Word, and we also need to apply our situation to what we have just read. We need to remember God's Word is alive and transforming. It is what can turn your life around. It is what will destroy the STRONGHOLD of food.

When we are saturated in the Word, demons become afraid you are going to quote those scriptures and they do not want to hear it because it will send them flying to somewhere else. Praise the Lord let them fly.

We need to go after the freedom, itself. Once we lay hold of real freedom, the STRONGHOLD of food will fall powerless at our feet. The devil will have no more ability to bind us than he had to bind Jesus. Remember, Jesus said to the Jews who had believed in Him:

> *If you abide in My Word hold fast to My teachings and live in accordance with them you are truly My disciples, and*

you will know the Truth and the Truth will set you free.

John 8:31-32

We need to get in the Word and not only read and meditate on what God says to us through His Word, but then we need to act on it as well.

> *For those who are according to the flesh and are controlled by its unholy desires set their minds on and pursue those things which gratify the flesh, but those who are according to the Spirit and are controlled by the desires of the Spirit set their minds on and seek those things which gratify the (Holy) Spirit.*
> *Romans 8:3*

We can't speak in negative fleshly terms and expect God to help us. We need a renewed way of thinking, in other words, we need to think the way God thinks and speak the words He tells us to speak about ourselves and stop listening and speaking what the enemy is whispering in our ear.

Don't be afraid to talk back to the enemy. God has given you that authority so stand up and use it!

> *Listen carefully; I have given you authority (that you now possess) to tread on serpents and scorpions, and (the ability to exercise authority) over all the power of the enemy (satan); and nothing will (in any way) harm you.*
> *Luke 10:19*

> *As a disciples of Christ I have the keys of the kingdom of heaven, and whatever I bind on earth is bound and*

whatever I loose is loosed.
                    Matthew 16:19

I submit myself to God, I resist the devil and He must flee. James 4:7

I've made it easy and listed some scriptures, now open your mouth and start speaking these into your life. Start telling the devil who you are and whose you are and know this in your heart and you will begin to have VICTORY thru SURRENDER!

WRITE ABOUT IT

Write some of your favorite scriptures here and really think about what God is saying to you through them.

CHAPTER TWENTY-EIGHT

The real battlefield

The real battlefield is always in your mind. If you have never read Joyce Meyer's book BATTLEFIELD OF THE MIND, you need to read it. Your mind, is where STRONGHOLDS get their beginning. The mind is the devils playground. What you say about yourself is what will determine your destiny. This is one of the reasons I ask you to tape yourself to see what kind of words come out of your mouth concerning you.

New life comes from a new mind and the way we think about ourselves. If you can destroy the negative thoughts you have going on (remember you have the power), you can destroy it in your life.

Your wrong doing is your reaction to unbelief. Do you believe that God wants to break the STRONGHOLD of food off your life? Are you fearing he will not do this for you? Fear is not believing what he promised will come to pass. The root of all love and goodness is belief. Belief on Him and that He wants nothing but good for you even if you do not think you deserve it, none of us deserve it, but He thinks you do. He loves you that much.

> *(Therefore beware) brethren, take care, least there*
> *Be in any one of you a wicked, unbelieving heart*
> *(which refuses to cleave to, trust in, and rely on*
> *Him), leading you to turn away and desert or stand*
> *aloof from the living God.*
> *Hebrews 3:12*

We just need to come to the end of ourselves so we can enter into God's strength. He is the only one who can break this STRONGHOLD that satan has set up in our minds. The Lord told Paul (different context) "My grace is sufficient for you, for My strength is made perfect in weakness," Paul responded, "When I am weak, then I am strong" (2 Cor. 12:9-10). We need the Lord's supernatural grace to be able to defeat the devil..

Sometimes we need to just acknowledge our weakness to God. He knows what it is but we need to speak it to Him. Just confess the following: "God I confess I am a food addict. Food has become my god. I lack the willpower to conquer this. I have tried time and time again to lose weight and to get into shape like I know in my heart you want me to do. But I keep failing on my own. Please help me, Father, and show me Your strength through my weakness!"

In Jesus you will have VICTORY thru SURRENDER. The longer you follow what he wants you to do to break this STRONGHOLD on food, the easier it will become, but we must become stronger in our soul first. We work so hard to shape up the outside of our bodies but sometimes we need to start on the inside, in our minds, heart, and attitude.

God does not want to withhold anything that is good for us. He wants to bless us. We are the only ones who can keep Him from doing what He wants to do for us. We need to tear down the old ways of thinking and doing from our old nature (our unsurrendered soul) and this will enlarge our capacity to receive our blessings.

God has given us powerful keys for dealing with our strongholds. Read and study these verses from Matthew;

> *I will give you the keys of the kingdom of heaven and whatever you bind (declare to be improper and unlawful) on earth must be what is already*

bound in heaven; and whatever you loose (declare lawful) on earth must be what is already loosed in heaven.
                    Matthew 16:19

Truly I tell you, whatever you forbid and declare to be improper and unlawful on earth must be what is already forbidden in heaven, and whatever you permit and declare proper and lawful on earth must be what is already permitted in heaven.
                    Matthew 18:18

Don't just read these verses, you need to meditate on them then apply its truths in your life. The more right choices you make the shorter your journey to VICTORY thru SURRENDER.

WRITE ABOUT IT

Do you fear God's promises will not come to pass for you?

Why?

CHAPTER TWENTY-NINE

I can do this

> *I have strength for all things in Christ who empowers me (I am ready for anything and equal to anything through Him who infuses inner strength in me; I am self-sufficient in Christ's sufficiency).*
> Philippians 4:13

You can either be loyal to your cravings or loyal to honoring God and allowing him to break that STRONGHOLD of food off your life.

> *"Do you not know that your body is a temple of the Holy Spirit, who is in you, whom you have received from God? You are not your own; you were bought at a price. Therefore honor God with your body"*
> 1Corinthians 6:19

If you came home from work tired and hungry and you are feeling weak and ready to just dive into eating anything to make you feel better, well, God's power is made perfect in weakness as we read earlier, weakness does not need to mean defeat. Actually it is an opportunity to experience the power of God first hand.

> *But he (Jesus) said to me, "My grace is sufficient for you, for my power is made perfect in weakness." Therefore I will boast all the more gladly about my weaknesses, so that Christ's power may rest on me. That is why, for Christ's sake, I delight in weakness, in insults, in hardships, in persecutions, in difficulties.*

For when I am weak, then I am strong.
                    2 Corinthians 12:9-10

Has this STRONGHOLD of food had a hold on you far too long? Have you struggled with overeating and eating the wrong foods when you are struggling in life? Do you keep going around the same mountain? Been there done that, and I don't know about you but enough is enough. Since everything I have ever tried had only worked for a short period of time, something is wrong. There has to be another way out. Then God began to show me and teach me about STRONGHOLDS of the devil. Then I had an awakening moment!

I was doing what man said with all the new diets, that was not God telling me. Then when he showed me about these STRONGHOLDS it all made sense. The devil teases us with all these new diets. He knows if we keep thinking about the food (which is what he wants) then we will certainly fail. I always said that there was one diet company I went to and it seems like all I did was think about food because I had to be constantly planning meals. Sound familiar?

Ruth Graham has something to say about going around that mountain too many times. In her book, Fear Not Tomorrow, God Is Already There;

> Either we can be victimized and become victims, or we can be victimized and rise above it. Often it is easier to Play the victim than take off our masks and ask for help. We get comfortable with our victim status. It becomes our identity and is hard to give up. The Israelites often played the victim card, and I love what God finally tells them "you have circled this mountain long enough. Now turn North (Deuteronomy 2:3(NASB)). Turn North! It's time to move on! Self-pity, fear, pride, and negativity paralyze us. Taking OFF our masks takes courage, but if

we don't do it, we will remain in our victim status and end up stunted.

Admitting you have a problem is the first step to allowing God to destroy your STRONGHOLD of food. Then you need to begin to make changes and for some, change can be difficult. Short time pleasure of a luscious desert or a salty snack you love, can seem like a quick fix, but that is all it is. But, God's Word is what will fill up your heart and satisfy you long term.

WRITE ABOUT IT

Are you ready to admit you have not trusted God in this area of your life?

Why are you still trying to do it yourself? It didn't work for you in the past, why to do think it will work now?

CHAPTER THIRTY

Silencing the cries

We are actually trying to silence the cries of a hungry soul. God is straight forward about His expectations and His promises:

> *You shall have no foreign god among you; you shall not bow down to an alien god. I am the LORD your God, who brought you up out of Egypt. Open wide your mouth and I will fill it.*
>
> *Psalm 81:9-10*

Nothing can satisfy like God's Word can!

STRONGHOLD has another meaning: a fortified place or a fortress. A place of survival or refuge. A stronghold into which people could go for shelter during a battle. This is how I feel about running to Jesus when tempted. He is my stronghold, not food.

Keep in His Word, keep running to Him, keep speaking His Word and watch the devil run..and watch your STRONGHOLD fall away. You will suddenly notice you are thinking differently about food and what you eat. It just becomes effortless. You may or may not lose weight that is not what this book is about, but I do believe you will because of all the changes you will make. But, I want to state again that is not what this book is about. God wanted this book written for you to recognize you have a STRONGHOLD in your life and that is why you are overweight and not feeling well. Just like he woke me up.

God bless you in your journey!

WRITE ABOUT IT

Open your heart to God now. Write about all you are feeling and thinking. Then release it ALL to God.

CHAPTER THIRTY-ONE

Final note

We need to get hold of the truth Jesus has for us. I know I have been redundant over several of the topics in this book, in other words, I have stated the same thing in different ways, so that you can get it. This is important. Not only that you get it, but you apply these truths, he has provided to be able to have VICTORY thru SURRENDER.

The devil will not give up because he does not want you to be successful. He is always there to whisper, "how many times have you tried to break this relationship with food and you failed? How many times have you cried? Admit it you are just a failure, you are still doing the same dumb things."

Our flesh will always fail! We cannot rely on our so called good intentions. It really is not about us trying harder. It is not a matter of us, it is a matter of HIM. In Him we can have VICTORY thru SURRENDER every time. Release your faith daily by thanking Him for breaking the STRONGHOLD food has had on you for so long.

When we first start releasing our faith, we may feel some doubt and unbelief, but keep going. You will suddenly notice you are believing them. We need to speak what we desire in our hearts.(see Mark 11:23-24). Also remember, we birth what we believe. So believe you have VICTORY thru SURRENDER and claim it NOW!

Food for thought (no pun intended)

>Praise will break strongholds.
>Complain and you remain.
>Praise and be changed.

>Send up vapors of praise. When you praise and worship, God shows up.

>Keep thanking God for His promises..

>Remember you are worth it, you are the righteousness of Christ. You are a child of the King. Just keep reminding the devil who you belong to. Stomp all over that devil!!!

SERVING OUR STRONGHOLDS WILL TAKE US

OUT

OF

GOD'S PRESENCE.

ABOUT THE AUTHOR

Pauline Porter has a Master's Degree in Christian Counseling and she is also a Life Coach. She specializes in helping women to stretch out of their comfort zones into the life God wants them to have.
She lives in Newburgh, IN with her husband Eddie and their lovable fur babies.

www.ingramcontent.com/pod-product-compliance
Lightning Source LLC
Chambersburg PA
CBHW022134080426
42734CB00006B/361